PRAYERSCRIPTS
Speaking God's Word Back To You

BRETHREN, PRAY FOR US

31 *Days of Prophetic Intercession for*

PASTORS AND SPIRITUAL LEADERS

CYRIL OPOKU

Brethren, Pray for Us: 31 Days of Prophetic Intercession for Pastors and Spiritual Leaders

Published by *Quest Publications*

ISBN: 978-1-988439-86-0

Cover design by *Quest Publications (questpublications@outlook.com)*

Unless otherwise indicated, all Scripture quotations are taken from the World English Bible WEB, which is in the public domain. For more information, visit: www.worldenglish.bible

This book is a work of devotional encouragement. It is not intended to replace biblical study, pastoral counsel, or professional therapy.

Printed in the United States of America.

First Edition: September 2025

For more books like this, visit *PrayerScripts:* https://prayerscripts.org

CONTENTS

DEDICATION

T his book is lovingly and prayerfully dedicated to the pastors who have shaped my Christian journey in ways words can scarcely capture:

To REV. (RTD) FRANCIS NYARKO—it was under your preaching that I first heard the voice of Christ calling me. Your unwavering passion for souls and your faithful oversight laid the foundation of my walk with God. Through your ministry, I learned not only to know the Lord but also to serve His church with reverence and joy.

To the late REV. JOSEPH OSEI-AMOAH—your mentorship marked a turning point in my life. You saw potential in me long before I saw it in myself. Under your guidance, I stepped into church leadership for the first time and began the journey of ministerial training. Though you have joined the cloud of witnesses, your legacy of faith and discipleship continues to live on in me.

To REV. ISAAC DE-GRAFT TAKYI—you opened my eyes to the spiritual gift of leadership and were the first to commission me to serve as a pastor. Your belief in me, your encouragement, and your push toward deeper theological study have forever shaped my calling and ministry path.

This work is a tribute to your spiritual labor, love, and lasting impact on my life.

PREFACE

"Brethren, pray for us." — 1 Thessalonians 5:25 WEB

Those four simple words from the Apostle Paul have echoed in my heart for years. They carry weight, urgency, and humility. The great apostle—mighty in revelation, fearless in mission, and unwavering in faith—still paused to plead for prayer. He understood something that many overlook: spiritual leaders, no matter how anointed, cannot fulfill their calling alone.

Over the years, I have watched pastors and ministers pour themselves out on the altar of service—preaching, counseling, praying, leading—often carrying burdens no one sees. Behind the sermons and smiles are real battles, private struggles, and spiritual warfare few can imagine. Yet the Kingdom advances because they keep standing.

"Brethren, Pray for Us" is my invitation to you to stand in the gap for them. Over thirty-one days, you will join prophetic intercessions covering every area of their lives—strength, protection, wisdom, family, health, and Kingdom impact. My heart is that as you pray, Heaven will respond with power, and pastors everywhere will rise with fresh anointing, divine covering, and unstoppable courage to fulfill their God-given assignments.

Let's lift their arms together.

Laboring in Prayer with You,
Cyril O. *(Toronto, September 2025)*

HOW TO USE THIS BOOK

This book is designed as a daily companion to guide you into a prophetic lifestyle of prayer. This is a prayer journey meant to position you to walk in the fullness of God's promises. Here's how to make the most of it:

1. Dedicate a Daily Time:

Set aside a consistent time each day to engage with the prayer for that day. Treat this as sacred time with God, where distractions are minimized, and your heart is fully focused on communion with Him. Ten to twenty minutes daily is sufficient to meditate on the Scripture, pray, and receive revelation.

2. Begin with Scripture Reflection:

Each day begins with a carefully selected Scripture. Read it slowly, meditate on its meaning, and let the Holy Spirit illuminate how it applies to your life. Allow the Word to penetrate your spirit and prepare you to pray from a place of faith and expectancy.

3. Pray the Guided Prayer:

Use the prayer provided as a framework, allowing it to resonate with your own words and personal circumstances. Speak each declaration with authority and confidence, fully believing that God is at work. You may also pause to personalize the prayer for your specific family, career, or ministry needs.

- **Make It Personal**

  These prayers are written in the first person so you can make them your own. Speak them aloud, inserting the names of your family members, your workplace, your church, or your city where applicable. The more you personalize the prayer, the more you will sense its power shaping your reality.

- **Pray with Authority**

  These are not timid requests; they are bold decrees. Lift your voice as a covenant child of God, covered by the blood of Jesus and backed by heaven's authority. When you pray, do so with confidence that Christ has already won the victory on your behalf.

- **Leave Room for the Holy Spirit**

  These written prayers are a guide, not a limit. As you pray, pause to listen. The Holy Spirit may give you prophetic words, insights, or specific instructions. Follow His lead. Allow Him to expand the prayer, add declarations, or guide you into deeper intercession.

4. Journal Your Insights:

Keep a notebook or journal to record any thoughts, revelations, or confirmations you receive during prayer. Writing down what God speaks to you helps solidify understanding and creates a record of breakthrough and growth over time.

5. Repeat as Needed:

Some prayers or themes may need to be revisited multiple times. Answer to prayer is progressive; the more you engage with these prayers in faith, the greater the manifestation in your life and household. You can return to this book at any season to reinforce your victory and dominion.

6. Live in Expectancy:

Prayer is only one part of walking in enlargement—your actions, faith, and obedience amplify the power of these prayers. Move boldly into opportunities, embrace the doors God opens, and live with a confident expectation that God is answering your prayer beyond what you can see or imagine.

By following this guide daily, you will cultivate a lifestyle of prayer and kingdom impact. Let this book be your companion as you step into the new dimensions God has destined for you.

INTRODUCTION

Prayer changes everything. When God's people lift their voices on behalf of others, heaven responds in power. Yet too often, one group stands at the very center of spiritual battles while remaining at the edges of our intercession: our pastors and spiritual leaders. Week after week, they pour out their hearts, carry the weight of souls, and contend for the Kingdom in prayer, teaching, and shepherding. And yet, many of them press on quietly, sometimes under heavy spiritual, emotional, and even physical burdens that few ever see.

This book, *Brethren, Pray for Us: 31 Days of Prophetic Intercession for Pastors and Spiritual Leaders*, is a call to change that. It is an invitation to pick up the mantle of prophetic intercession and stand in the gap for the men and women God has set over His flock. For thirty-one days, you will journey through targeted, Spirit-led prayers covering every area of a pastor's life and ministry—from spiritual strength and protection to family health, divine wisdom, and Kingdom expansion. Each prayer flows from Scripture, carrying the fire of God's Word and the urgency of the Spirit.

Here, you will not find casual words or routine prayers. These are prophetic declarations, birthed from the heart of intercession, designed to break strongholds, release blessing, and call forth divine intervention for pastors everywhere. Each week carries a distinct theme, guiding you to pray with clarity, passion, and purpose. By the end of this journey, your pastor—and indeed, spiritual leaders across the globe—will be covered in prayer as never before.

So come with expectation. Let faith rise in your heart as you declare God's Word over His servants. Together, we will lift their arms, strengthen their hearts, and advance the Kingdom on our knees.

WEEK 1: SPIRITUAL STRENGTH & FRESH ANOINTING

When the weight of ministry grows heavy, God's strength becomes the lifeline for every spiritual leader. Pastors and ministers carry the eternal burden of souls, often pressing forward while fighting unseen battles. This week, we intercede passionately for a fresh outpouring of strength and anointing upon them. As Moses' hands were lifted in battle, so shall our prayers uphold the arms of those leading God's people. We will call forth supernatural endurance, resilience in trials, and divine empowerment to minister with boldness and power. Every prayer will birth renewed strength and a fresh oil of the Spirit to keep them burning brightly for the Kingdom.

DAY 1

EMPOWERED FOR BOLD UTTERANCE

"With all prayer and requests, praying at all times in the Spirit, and being watchful to this end in all perseverance and requests for all the saints: on my behalf, that utterance may be given to me in opening my mouth, to make known with boldness the mystery of the Good News, for which I am an ambassador in chains; that in it I may speak boldly, as I ought to speak."
— Ephesians 6:18–20 WEB

Lord of Hosts, Mighty One of Israel, I stand before You as an intercessor today, calling upon the power of Heaven for my pastor and for all those who carry the sacred flame of the Gospel across the earth. Father, I invoke the strength of Your Spirit over their lives, that they may be clothed with boldness and courage to speak the mysteries of Christ unhindered by fear or opposition.

I declare, O God, that no chain of intimidation, no barrier of persecution, and no wall of resistance will silence the voices of Your servants. I decree that tongues of fire will rest upon them afresh, filling them with heavenly utterance and divine clarity. Let the Good News flow from their lips with signs and wonders following.

Holy Spirit, grant them perseverance in prayer and resilience in the face of trials. Strengthen their inner man that they will not grow weary in well-doing. Surround them with angelic hosts as they march forward with the Gospel torch into dark territories.

Father, as they open their mouths, let wisdom and grace drip from their words like honey from the comb, transforming hearts, breaking chains, and bringing the lost into the kingdom of light. Let the oil of gladness rest upon their heads as they speak of Christ crucified, risen, and reigning forevermore.

I intercede that every minister of the Gospel will walk in divine authority, fearless and unwavering, declaring Your truth to the nations. Let them speak as oracles of God, with a holy fire that cannot be quenched.

In Jesus' name, Amen.

DAY 2

STRENGTHENED WITH DIVINE MIGHT

"For this cause, we also, since the day we heard this, don't cease praying and making requests for you, that you may be filled with the knowledge of his will in all spiritual wisdom and understanding, that you may walk worthily of the Lord, to please him in all respects, bearing fruit in every good work, and increasing in the knowledge of God, strengthened with all power, according to the might of his glory, for all endurance and perseverance with joy."
— Colossians 1:9–11 WEB

O Father of Lights, the Source of all wisdom and might, I lift up my pastor and every servant who labors in Your vineyard. With fervency of spirit, I cry out for a fresh infilling of divine wisdom, that they may discern Your will with clarity and precision in every assignment You have entrusted to them.

Lord, I decree that they shall walk worthy of the calling with which You have called them. May their lives be living epistles, bringing pleasure to You in all things. Let their words bear fruit, their counsel bring direction, and their steps align perfectly with Your eternal purposes.

I call forth the strength of Heaven upon them, that they may be fortified with all might according to Your glorious power. Father, let endurance rise within their hearts like an unshakable pillar, that in times of trial they will not break, in moments of warfare they will not retreat.

I declare that joy shall be their portion even in seasons of testing. Let the oil of gladness flow through their spirits, refreshing them from the inside out. May they mount up with wings as eagles, refusing to faint or grow weary as they carry the banner of the Gospel to every corner of the earth.

Father, surround every minister with Your presence like a wall of fire, granting them strength to fulfill Your mandate with excellence and grace.

In Jesus' name, Amen.

DAY 3

DELIVERED FROM EVIL MEN

"Finally, brothers, pray for us, that the word of the Lord may spread rapidly and be glorified, even as also with you; and that we may be delivered from unreasonable and evil men; for not all have faith."
— 2 Thessalonians 3:1–2 WEB

Almighty Deliverer, the One who shatters the plans of the wicked, I stand in the gap today for my pastor and all who bear the Word of life. I decree that the Gospel of Christ shall run swiftly through their ministries, unhindered and unstoppable, to the glory of Your great Name.

Father, I lift up a shield of intercession around them, declaring divine protection from all who oppose the truth. Deliver them, O Lord, from the snares of unreasonable and wicked men, from voices of deception, from the plots of darkness, and from every spirit that seeks to silence the Gospel.

I decree that no weapon formed against Your servants shall prosper. Let every tongue that rises against them in judgment be condemned. As they proclaim the Word, let the Spirit of truth accompany them with miracles, signs, and wonders, silencing the lies of the enemy.

Lord, I call for angelic reinforcements to surround every minister of the Gospel, thwarting the agendas of wickedness. May the Word of the Lord spread like wildfire through nations, cities, and villages, until every heart has heard the name of Jesus.

I declare that courage shall rise within them like a mighty lion. No opposition, no criticism, and no persecution shall deter them from the holy assignment You have given them. Let the banner of Christ fly high over every territory where they labor for Your kingdom.

In Jesus' name, Amen.

DAY 4

THE SPIRIT OF THE LORD

"The Lord Yahweh's Spirit is on me; because Yahweh has anointed me to preach good news to the humble. He has sent me to bind up the brokenhearted, to proclaim liberty to the captives, and release to those who are bound; to proclaim the year of Yahweh's favor and the day of vengeance of our God; to comfort all who mourn; to provide for those who mourn in Zion, to give to them a garland for ashes, the oil of joy for mourning, the garment of praise for the spirit of heaviness; that they may be called trees of righteousness, the planting of Yahweh, that he may be glorified."
— Isaiah 61:1–3 WEB

Spirit of the Living God, fall afresh upon my pastor and upon every laborer in Your harvest field. Let the same anointing that rested upon Christ flow without measure upon their lives today.

Father, I decree that they shall preach good news with power to the humble and the brokenhearted. Through their words, let captives be set free, chains be broken, and hearts be healed. Let the anointing destroy every yoke of oppression and usher multitudes into the glorious liberty of the sons of God.

Lord, I release a fresh oil of gladness upon their spirits. Where heaviness once lingered, let songs of praise break forth like a mighty river. Where weariness has weighed them down, let divine strength arise from within them, turning mourning into dancing and sorrow into shouts of victory.

I declare that as they proclaim the year of the Lord's favor, entire cities shall encounter the outpouring of Your Spirit. Let their ministries become oases of healing, deliverance, and restoration, bringing hope to the hopeless and joy to the desolate.

Father, plant them as trees of righteousness whose roots run deep into Your presence. May their lives glorify You continually, standing tall and unshakable through every storm of life and ministry.

In Jesus' name, Amen.

DAY 5

BOLDNESS TO SPEAK YOUR WORD

"Now, Lord, look at their threats, and grant to your servants to speak your word with all boldness, while you stretch out your hand to heal; and that signs and wonders may be done through the name of your holy Servant Jesus."
— Acts 4:29–31 WEB

Mighty God, the One who answers by fire, I lift up my pastor and every minister of the Gospel before Your throne of grace today. Lord, behold the threats, the oppositions, and the voices of intimidation that rise against Your servants, and stretch forth Your mighty hand to silence the enemy.

I declare that fresh boldness shall arise within their spirits like a holy flame. Let them proclaim Your Word fearlessly, unmoved by danger, criticism, or persecution. May they be clothed with courage from on high, speaking with divine authority that pierces the darkness and sets captives free.

Father, as they speak, let Your healing power flow mightily through their hands. Let blind eyes open, deaf ears hear, broken bodies be restored, and weary hearts be made whole. Confirm their words with signs and wonders that testify of the risen Christ.

I decree that their ministries shall be rivers of revival, transforming entire communities with the power of the Gospel. As they open their mouths, let the heavens back their words with miracles that no man can deny, bringing glory to the name of Jesus alone.

Lord, fill every pastor, prophet, teacher, and evangelist with the Spirit of boldness and unwavering faith, that Your kingdom may advance in power and glory throughout the nations of the earth.

In Jesus' name, Amen.

DAY 6

STRIVING TOGETHER IN PRAYER

> "Now I beg you, brothers, by our Lord Jesus Christ, and by
> the love of the Spirit, that you strive together with me in
> your prayers to God for me, that I may be delivered from
> those who are disobedient in Judea, and that my service
> which I have for Jerusalem may be acceptable to the saints;
> that I may come to you in joy by the will of God, and
> together with you, find rest."
> — Romans 15:30–32 WEB

Father of Mercy, I come before You today to labor in the spirit for
my pastor and for all who faithfully proclaim the Gospel of Christ.
I join my faith with theirs, lifting up a cry of intercession that will
shake the heavens and bring forth divine intervention on their
behalf.

Lord, I decree that they shall be delivered from disobedient and
hostile men, from wicked plots and demonic strategies that rise
against the work of Christ. I cover their lives, their families, and
their ministries with the blood of Jesus, declaring divine protection
on every side.

I call forth favor upon their service, that their labor in the kingdom
will be acceptable and fruitful among the saints. Let doors of
ministry open wide before them, bringing joy and refreshing as
they fulfill the will of God with excellence and grace.

Father, I declare rest over their minds, bodies, and spirits. May they not labor under the weight of constant warfare but experience times of refreshing in Your presence. Let joy spring up like a well within them, bringing renewal to every weary place in their souls.

Lord, unite the Body of Christ in fervent prayer for every servant of the Gospel, that together we may see revival fire sweep across nations until the glory of the Lord covers the earth as the waters cover the sea.

In Jesus' name, Amen.

DAY 7

BUILDING UP IN HOLY FAITH

"But you, beloved, keep building up yourselves on your most holy faith, praying in the Holy Spirit. Keep yourselves in God's love, looking for the mercy of our Lord Jesus Christ to eternal life."
— Jude 1:20–21 WEB

Holy and Righteous Father, I lift my voice today for my pastor and for all who labor in the Word and doctrine. I decree that they shall be continually built up in the most holy faith, rising strong in the spirit through ceaseless communion with You.

Lord, let the fire of prayer never burn out upon the altar of their hearts. May they pray in the Holy Spirit without ceasing, drawing strength, wisdom, and power from the wells of salvation. I declare that they will be saturated with Your presence, walking in unbroken fellowship with the Spirit of grace.

Father, I decree that they will be rooted and grounded in Your love, standing unshaken through every storm of life and ministry. Let the revelation of Your mercy and the hope of eternal life sustain them through seasons of trial and warfare.

I speak refreshing over their minds and bodies, that they may run and not grow weary, walk and not faint. May the joy of the Lord be their strength, and the peace of God guard their hearts and minds in Christ Jesus.

Lord, raise up a mighty generation of praying pastors and interceding ministers who will carry revival fire across the nations. Let them be carriers of glory, vessels of honor, and heralds of truth in this generation.

In Jesus' name, Amen.

WEEK 2: DIVINE PROTECTION & DELIVERANCE

Spiritual leaders stand on the frontlines of warfare, confronting powers of darkness while shepherding God's flock. Their safety and deliverance are vital for Kingdom advance. This week, our prayers rise like a shield around them—declaring angelic covering, deliverance from every snare, and protection from spiritual, emotional, and physical harm. We will cry out for God's hedge of fire around their lives, families, and ministries. No weapon formed against them will prosper, and every plan of the enemy will be utterly dismantled. As we intercede, Heaven's armies will surround them with divine preservation and supernatural victory on every side.

DAY 8

SAFE IN HIS SHADOW

He who dwells in the secret place of the Most High will rest in the shadow of the Almighty. I will say of Yahweh, "He is my refuge and my fortress; my God, in whom I trust." For he will deliver you from the snare of the fowler, and from the deadly pestilence.
— Psalm 91:1–3 WEB

Almighty Father, Commander of the angelic hosts and Refuge of the righteous, I come before You today with a heart ablaze in intercession for my pastor and every faithful servant of the Gospel across the nations. Lord, I declare that they abide under Your shadow where no evil hand can reach, where no demonic assignment can prevail, and where no weapon of hell can find its mark.

By faith, I declare them hidden in Your pavilion, O God. May the secret place of Your Presence be their continual dwelling, a place where every trap of the enemy dissolves into nothingness. I plead the blood of Jesus over their lives, homes, families, and ministries, decreeing divine immunity against pestilence, spiritual arrows, and secret snares.

Father, surround them with walls of fire; let angelic sentinels stand guard at every gate of access into their lives. May Your Spirit frustrate every plot of darkness before it even takes form. I lift pastors, evangelists, teachers, prophets, and apostles into this same covering today, speaking divine escape from every snare set against their assignments.

I prophesy that no sudden destruction, no hidden danger, no unclean arrow shall prosper against them. They will live, thrive, and proclaim the works of the Lord unhindered because they are sealed in the covenant of divine protection.

In Jesus' name, Amen.

DAY 9

NO WEAPON SHALL PROSPER

No weapon that is formed against you will prevail; and you will condemn every tongue that rises against you in judgment. This is the heritage of Yahweh's servants, and their righteousness is of me," says Yahweh.
— Isaiah 54:17 WEB

Righteous Judge of all the earth, I stand before Your throne today, lifting up my pastor and every anointed servant laboring for the sake of Your Kingdom. I decree with Heaven's authority that every weapon of darkness aimed at them is shattered by the power of Your Word.

Lord, silence every tongue of accusation, every whispering spirit of slander, every counsel of darkness that seeks to cripple their influence or tarnish their testimony. Let Your judgment arise like fire, consuming every plot against their lives, families, and ministries. Cause every malicious arrow to return empty to its sender, for they carry the heritage of Your covenant protection.

I speak life, strength, and courage over them. No illness, no spiritual assault, no demonic siege will overthrow the work of their hands. The Church of Jesus Christ marches on under Your banner, and every servant leading the charge shall stand in victory.

Father, establish their righteousness as a shining light before the nations. May the fragrance of Christ's triumph flow from them unhindered, and may their words pierce the darkness with the authority of Heaven.

Let this decree echo across borders and continents: no satanic weapon will prevail against the servants of God. They rise above every storm, marked as untouchable vessels of divine assignment.

In Jesus' name, Amen.

DAY 10

EYES TO SEE THE INVISIBLE

He answered, "Don't be afraid, for those who are with us are more than those who are with them." Elisha prayed, and said, "Yahweh, please open his eyes, that he may see." Yahweh opened the young man's eyes, and he saw; and behold, the mountain was full of horses and chariots of fire around Elisha.
— 2 Kings 6:16–17 WEB

O Lord of Hosts, the God who surrounds His people with chariots of fire, I cry out today for my pastor and every laborer in the Gospel vineyard. Open their eyes, Lord, to behold the unseen armies standing guard around them, the celestial warriors stationed to ensure no scheme of darkness prevails.

I declare that fear shall not grip their hearts, for the God who commands angelic battalions fights for them. Father, let every pastor weary from battles, every missionary pressed by opposition, every leader standing in hostile territories receive fresh courage as Heaven's armies encamp about them.

Lord, I speak divine reassurance into their spirits: they are not alone. The fire that guarded Elisha now blazes around them. Let the invisible become reality—tangible deliverances, miraculous escapes, and testimonies of divine intervention manifest in their ministries.

Where threats rise against their lives, let the overwhelming might of Your heavenly host scatter adversaries. Let ministers of the Gospel move in boldness, knowing that the God of angel armies fights unseen battles on their behalf.

I prophesy that victory, not defeat, shall be their portion. The Kingdom shall advance, and the servants of Christ shall be preserved by the fire of God encamping round about them.

In Jesus' name, Amen.

DAY 11

KEEPER OF ISRAEL

I will lift up my eyes to the hills. Where does my help come from? My help comes from Yahweh, who made heaven and earth. He will not allow your foot to be moved. He who keeps you will not slumber. Behold, he who keeps Israel will neither slumber nor sleep. Yahweh is your keeper. Yahweh is your shade on your right hand. The sun will not harm you by day, nor the moon by night. Yahweh will keep you from all evil. He will keep your soul. Yahweh will keep your going out and your coming in, from this time forward, and forever more.
— Psalm 121:1–8 WEB

Ever-wakeful Keeper of Israel, my heart overflows with intercession today for my pastor and every shepherd faithfully tending Your flock. Lord, You neither slumber nor sleep, and so I declare that no evil shall find access to them by day or by night.

I call upon You, Maker of heaven and earth, to preserve their steps. Let no misstep, no sudden accident, no spiritual ambush befall them. Be the shade at their right hand, shielding them from every arrow of fatigue, burnout, and hidden attack.

Father, as they travel on Kingdom assignments, as they minister across cities and nations, I decree divine preservation upon their journeys. Keep them from every plan of violence, every hidden danger on the road, every threat in the air.

Let this same covering spread across pastors in villages, prophets in cities, teachers in seminaries, missionaries in hostile lands—none shall be uncovered, none left vulnerable, for the Keeper of Israel shields them all.

I proclaim that their souls, bodies, and ministries are secured under eternal watchfulness. They will fulfill destiny, finish their course, and testify of divine keeping in all seasons.

In Jesus' name, Amen.

DAY 12

RESCUED FROM EVERY EVIL

But the Lord stood by me, and strengthened me, that through me the message might be fully proclaimed, and that all the Gentiles might hear; and I was delivered out of the mouth of the lion. And the Lord will deliver me from every evil work, and will preserve me for his heavenly Kingdom; to him be the glory forever and ever. Amen.
— 2 Timothy 4:17–18 WEB

Mighty Deliverer, the One who rescues from the mouth of lions, I lift up my pastor and every voice declaring the Gospel across nations. Lord, stand by them as You stood by Paul; let Your strength fill them when human help fails.

I decree divine rescue from every evil work—plots of death, traps of compromise, subtle snares of the enemy. Lord, preserve their minds from discouragement, their hearts from betrayal, their bodies from affliction, and their ministries from destruction.

May the message of Christ thunder unhindered through their lips, reaching tribes, cities, and nations without interference from the powers of darkness. As they labor under threats, I speak divine boldness and angelic protection around them.

Father, preserve their lives for Your heavenly Kingdom. Let no scheme cut short their assignments; let no weapon silence their witness. Crown their years with strength, victories, and souls won for Christ.

Across continents, I decree deliverance for pastors in danger, missionaries in war zones, and evangelists in hostile lands. The Lord delivers, the Lord preserves, the Lord upholds His servants until their race is complete.

In Jesus' name, Amen.

DAY 13

ANGELIC ENCAMPMENT

The angel of Yahweh encamps around those who fear him,
and delivers them.
— Psalm 34:7 WEB

Captain of the Lord's hosts, I lift my voice today over my pastor and every devoted servant laboring in Your harvest fields. Lord, release angelic armies to encamp round about them as a living shield of deliverance.

Where demonic forces plot, let angelic warriors stand guard. Where human enemies conspire, let Heaven's messengers intercept. I declare that no scheme of darkness will outwit the divine protection surrounding Your servants.

Father, let there be supernatural interventions—accidents averted, bullets deflected, diseases halted, storms stilled—by the hands of ministering angels assigned to the heirs of salvation.

Lord, fill their homes, pulpits, and mission fields with angelic presence. May discouragement, weariness, and fear flee as the atmosphere of Heaven surrounds them continually.

I speak this over pastors in cities and jungles alike: the angel of the Lord encamps around you; therefore, you are delivered from every snare, every danger, every terror of the night or arrow of the day.

Let the Church arise knowing her leaders are divinely shielded, advancing in safety to fulfill the Great Commission. In Jesus' name, Amen.

DAY 14

WALL OF FIRE

For I, says Yahweh, will be to her a wall of fire around it,
and I will be the glory in the middle of her.
— Zechariah 2:5 WEB

Consuming Fire, glorious Defender of Your people, I raise a prophetic cry today for my pastor and all who lead in the household of faith. Lord, surround them with walls not of stone, but of blazing fire that no enemy can penetrate.

Let this wall repel sickness, scatter demonic forces, and blind every monitoring spirit seeking access into their lives and ministries. May this divine fire burn day and night, leaving no gap for darkness to invade.

Father, be the glory within them—renewing their strength, refreshing their spirits, filling them with wisdom and courage. Let Your presence within be their continual light, and Your fire around be their unbreakable defense.

I decree over missionaries in dangerous territories, over pastors facing persecution, over leaders carrying heavy Kingdom mandates: the Lord Himself is your wall of fire; no force of hell shall breach His defense.

Let this fire consume every curse, nullify every enchantment, and render powerless every scheme launched against Your servants. They shall stand untouchable because the glory of the Lord fills their midst, and the fire of the Lord surrounds their borders. In Jesus' name, Amen.

WEEK 3: WISDOM, GUIDANCE & VISION

Leadership demands more than human insight; it requires Heaven's direction. Pastors and ministers need divine wisdom to lead God's people, navigate challenges, and discern spiritual seasons. This week, we will intercede for clarity of vision, sensitivity to the Spirit's leading, and wisdom beyond natural understanding. Our prayers will call forth prophetic foresight, strategic direction, and divine creativity for Kingdom advancement. Like the sons of Issachar who understood the times, spiritual leaders will receive the guidance needed to lead effectively, build faithfully, and walk in alignment with Heaven's agenda for the Church and the nations.

DAY 15

OVERFLOWING WISDOM FROM ABOVE

"But if any of you lacks wisdom, let him ask of God, who gives to all liberally and without reproach; and it will be given to him."
— James 1:5 WEB

O Ancient of Days, Fountain of Eternal Wisdom, I lift my voice as an intercessor standing in the gap for my pastor, the shepherd You have set over my life. Lord, You are the God who gives wisdom generously, without scolding or withholding, and today I prophetically declare that a new measure of divine wisdom is resting upon Your servant.

Father, as Solomon asked and received a wise and understanding heart to lead Your people, I decree that my pastor shall not walk in the frailty of human reasoning but in the overflowing wisdom of the Spirit. Every decision, every sermon, every counsel shall be birthed out of the deep well of Your divine insight. Let there be no confusion in the path before him, for You have promised to give wisdom liberally to all who ask.

Lord, I tear down the voice of doubt and silence every whisper of the enemy that seeks to cloud his discernment. I pray that the Spirit of wisdom and revelation will flood his mind, granting clarity where there was uncertainty, and direction where there was hesitation.

And beyond my pastor, I stretch my intercession over every minister in the Body of Christ. May the Church of the Living God rise in a new dimension of prophetic wisdom to navigate these end times with accuracy and power. Crown them with wisdom that speaks from eternity into time.

Father, let this wisdom flow like a river, shaping decisions, guiding visions, and perfecting purposes. None shall stumble in darkness, for Your wisdom shall be their light.

In Jesus' name, Amen.

DAY 16

Divine Paths Made Straight

"Trust in Yahweh with all your heart, and don't lean on
your own understanding. In all your ways acknowledge
him, and he will make your paths straight."
— Proverbs 3:5–6 WEB

O Lord of Heaven and Earth, I lift my heart in reverent awe before
Your throne, declaring that my pastor's life and ministry are
anchored in Your perfect wisdom. You are the One who straightens
crooked paths, the Navigator of destinies, the God who makes ways
in the wilderness. Today, I invoke Your Word over him, that he shall
trust wholly and fully in You.

Lord, I decree that no earthly reasoning or human counsel shall
overshadow Your divine leading in his life. Cause his heart to be
steadfast in reliance upon Your Spirit. Let every path before him be
illuminated by the radiance of Your presence, leaving no room for
confusion or delay.

Abba Father, I prophetically speak alignment into his ministry
vision, that he shall acknowledge You in every plan, every project,
every sermon, and every decision. May his trust in You birth
precision, direction, and favor. May the wisdom from above chart
a straight course for the mandate You've committed to him.

Lord, extend this intercession over every shepherd and minister in
Your Body. In a world filled with conflicting voices, make them

sensitive to Yours alone. Deliver them from the snare of human wisdom that lacks eternal perspective.

I decree that Your Church shall not grope in darkness, for You, O Lord, are the Shepherd who guides with unfailing love. Every crooked place becomes straight, every valley lifted, and every mountain made low before the counsel of Your will.

In Jesus' name, Amen.

DAY 17

HEARING THE VOICE BEHIND

"When you turn to the right hand, and when you turn to
the left, your ears will hear a voice behind you, saying,
'This is the way. Walk in it.'"
— Isaiah 30:21 WEB

O Lord God Almighty, the Voice that thunders over many waters,
today I cry out for my pastor, that he will walk in the assurance of
Your unfailing guidance. Let his spirit be tuned like a trumpet to
the sound of Your voice.

Father, I decree that in every decision, in every vision You birth
through him, he will hear clearly the divine whisper saying, "This
is the way, walk in it." Silence the noise of human reasoning, mute
the clamor of fear, and break the grip of uncertainty. May his ears
be sharpened to discern the direction of heaven over the
distractions of earth.

Lord, let Your voice become the compass that steadies his path,
ensuring he does not turn aside to the left or to the right. Align his
heart with the cadence of Your Spirit. May he never run ahead of
Your timing nor lag behind Your leading.

And Father, let this same grace rest upon every minister across the
nations. In this hour where deception seeks to derail many, may
Your servants hear Your instructions with precision. Cause Your
Word to be the loudest sound in their spirits.

I declare that divine direction is released upon the Church, for where Your voice leads, victory follows. The enemy's snares are broken, and the pathways of righteousness are revealed for Your glory.

In Jesus' name, Amen.

DAY 18

TREASURES OF WISDOM UNLOCKED

"...that their hearts may be comforted, they being knit together in love, and gaining all riches of the full assurance of understanding, that they may know the mystery of God, both of the Father and of Christ, in whom all the treasures of wisdom and knowledge are hidden."
— Colossians 2:2–3 WEB

O King of Glory, Possessor of all wisdom and knowledge, I lift up my pastor before Your throne, declaring that every hidden treasure of divine insight shall be unlocked over his life. Lord, You are the Keeper of mysteries, the Revealer of secrets, and the Source of all understanding.

I prophesy that my pastor shall not walk in partial light, but in the full assurance of understanding. Cause his heart to be anchored in the depths of Christ, where the treasures of wisdom and knowledge reside. Let his ministry radiate divine intelligence that confounds the adversary and glorifies the name of Jesus.

Lord, knit his heart in love with Your Spirit and with those You have called him to serve. Let wisdom flow through relationships, decisions, visions, and assignments. Break the power of confusion, shatter the chains of indecision, and grant him strategies from the throne room of heaven.

And Father, I extend this intercession to every laborer in Your vineyard. May Your ministers receive the spirit of revelation to rightly divide the Word of Truth, to lead with precision, and to build according to heavenly blueprints.

Let the Church arise in prophetic insight, moving in alignment with the mysteries of the Kingdom, demonstrating wisdom that turns the hearts of men toward Christ.

In Jesus' name, Amen.

DAY 19

VISION FOR THE APPOINTED TIME

"Yahweh answered me, 'Write the vision, and make it plain on tablets, that he who runs may read it. For the vision is yet for the appointed time, and it hurries toward the end, and won't prove false. Though it takes time, wait for it; because it will surely come. It won't delay.'"
— Habakkuk 2:2–3 WEB

Mighty God, Author of destiny, I lift my voice with holy fervor on behalf of my pastor. You are the God who speaks vision into the hearts of men, the One who appoints times and seasons for Your divine purposes to unfold.

I decree that fresh vision is being inscribed upon the tablets of his spirit. No longer shall the call or direction be blurry; the Word of the Lord shall be plain, powerful, and prophetic. Every runner assigned to the vision will see it clearly and run with unwavering faith.

Lord, I declare that my pastor shall not faint in the waiting season. Even when the vision tarries, grant him grace to stand in faith, knowing it will speak at the appointed time. Frustration, weariness, and discouragement shall not swallow his zeal, for the Word of the Lord cannot fail.

Father, let this prophetic anointing for clarity and endurance fall upon every leader in Your Church. Let visionaries arise across the nations, building according to Your timing, refusing to compromise under pressure.

I decree the enemy shall not derail divine purposes. The vision shall speak, the appointed time shall manifest, and the name of the Lord shall be glorified in every nation through obedient servants.

In Jesus' name, Amen.

DAY 20

REVEALED BY THE SPIRIT

"But as it is written, 'Things which an eye didn't see, and an ear didn't hear, which didn't enter into the heart of man, these God has prepared for those who love him.' But to us, God revealed them through the Spirit. For the Spirit searches all things, yes, the deep things of God."
— 1 Corinthians 2:9–10 WEB

Spirit of the Living God, today I cry out for my pastor, that he may walk in the deep things of God. You are the One who unveils what human eyes cannot see and human minds cannot comprehend.

I decree that the mysteries You have prepared for his life and ministry will no longer be concealed. By the Spirit's illumination, secrets buried in the depths of eternity shall be revealed for divine assignment and Kingdom advancement.

Lord, take him beyond surface understanding. Open his spiritual eyes to see strategies from heaven, his ears to hear the whispers of eternity, and his heart to conceive the fullness of Your plans. Let there be a flood of divine revelation that shifts his ministry into supernatural dimensions.

And Father, stretch this mantle over every pastor and minister in Your Church. Break the barriers of human reasoning, demolish the walls of natural limitation, and raise leaders who carry heaven's intelligence to confront earth's challenges.

May the Body of Christ rise in prophetic depth, flowing with insight that comes only from the Spirit who searches the deep things of God.

In Jesus' name, Amen.

DAY 21

TEACH ME YOUR PATHS

"Show me your ways, Yahweh. Teach me your paths.
Guide me in your truth, and teach me, for you are the God
of my salvation; I wait for you all day long."
— Psalm 25:4–5 WEB

O Lord, Shepherd of Israel, I lift up my pastor to You, crying out for divine instruction and heavenly guidance. You are the God who teaches, who leads, who directs paths into righteousness for Your name's sake.

I decree that my pastor shall not stumble in the darkness of uncertainty. Teach him Your ways, O Lord, ways higher than the wisdom of men. Lead him into the secret counsels of Your will, where truth flows like rivers of life, shaping vision, strategy, and destiny.

Father, I prophetically declare that his heart remains teachable before You. Pride shall not blind him, nor shall distraction silence the voice of Your Spirit. As he waits upon You, unveil the mysteries of Your Word and the blueprints of Your Kingdom.

Extend this intercession to every servant in the global Church. Raise leaders who sit at Your feet like Mary, receiving revelation that births transformation. Break the cycle of self-reliance, and teach Your ministers to depend wholly on Your Spirit's guidance.

Let Your truth light every path, Your wisdom govern every decision, and Your salvation become the anchor of every assignment. Lead Your shepherds in ways that please You, for where You guide, victory and fruitfulness follow.

In Jesus' name, Amen.

Week 4: Family, Health & Personal Refreshing

Behind the pulpit stands a person with real needs, emotions, and a family who shares the weight of ministry. Too often, pastors pour out endlessly yet struggle silently with exhaustion, health battles, or family pressures. This week, we lift them before the Lord for holistic restoration. Our prayers will speak healing over their bodies, peace over their homes, and joy over their hearts. We will cry out for seasons of refreshing where weariness breaks, health springs forth speedily, and families thrive in unity and strength. As they pour into others, may they be continually refilled with life, love, and divine wholeness.

DAY 22

PROSPERITY OF SOUL AND BODY

"Beloved, I pray that you may prosper in all things and be
healthy, even as your soul prospers."
— 3 John 1:2 WEB

O Lord, my Shield and my exceeding Great Reward, I lift my voice
in prophetic decree over my pastor, the shepherd You have set over
my life, and over all Your faithful servants across the earth. Today,
I stand in the gap as an intercessor, releasing Your Word into their
lives, declaring that they will prosper in all things and walk in
divine health as their souls flourish in You.

Father, I cry out for supernatural strength, divine vitality, and
physical renewal over every servant of the Gospel who pours out
day and night in service to You. May every trace of weariness be
swallowed by Your resurrection life. Where sickness has attempted
to invade their bodies, let the healing power of Jesus' stripes prevail,
restoring vigor and energy.

Lord, let every burden weighing on their minds be lifted. Flood
their souls with peace and clarity. As their spirits thrive in Your
presence, let every other area of their lives—family, finances,
emotions—align with heaven's prosperity. May their children rise
like olive plants around their tables, their spouses flourish, and their
homes overflow with joy and abundance.

I decree open heavens over them. Let doors of provision swing
wide, opportunities for rest and refreshing multiply, and

relationships sent by You bring comfort and strength. Wherever there has been lack, release abundance. Where there has been warfare, release victory.

Today, I declare that my pastor and every minister of the Gospel will live untouchable under the covenant blood of Jesus—prosperous in soul, mind, body, and spirit.

In Jesus' name, Amen.

DAY 23

BLESSED HOUSEHOLD HERITAGE

"Blessed is everyone who fears Yahweh, who walks in his
ways. For you will eat the labor of your hands. You will be
happy, and it will be well with you. Your wife will be as a
fruitful vine in the innermost parts of your house; your
children like olive plants, around your table."
— Psalm 128:1–3 WEB

Almighty God, Covenant-Keeper, I raise a cry of intercession for
my pastor and for every servant laboring in Your vineyard. Today,
I declare over them the blessing of the Lord that makes rich and
adds no sorrow. Let the fear of the Lord anchor their hearts, guiding
every step they take in righteousness and integrity.

Father, command Your blessing upon the labor of their hands. Let
every sermon preached, every prayer lifted, every hour spent
counseling and caring for Your people bring forth eternal fruit. May
their lives overflow with joy unspeakable, peace unshakable, and
favor undeniable.

I decree that their marriages will be marked by harmony, love, and
mutual honor. Their spouses will be strengthened in faith, their
homes will be sanctuaries of divine presence, and their children will
be arrows in the hand of the Mighty God—sharp, strong, and
destined for kingdom exploits.

Where the enemy has tried to sow division, Lord, release unity.
Where there has been fatigue, bring refreshing. Let laughter fill

their homes, songs of thanksgiving fill their nights, and testimonies of breakthrough rise continually from their lips.

Today, I prophetically call forth a legacy of blessing upon their generations. Their children will be taught of the Lord, their peace will be great, and their homes will be living testimonies of Your faithfulness.

In Jesus' name, Amen.

DAY 24

RENEWED STRENGTH LIKE EAGLES

"He gives power to the weak. He increases the strength of him who has no might. Even the youths faint and get weary, and the young men utterly fall; but those who wait for Yahweh will renew their strength. They will mount up with wings like eagles. They will run, and not be weary. They will walk, and not faint."
— Isaiah 40:29–31 WEB

Everlasting God, the Strength of Israel, I come before You today as an intercessor for my pastor and for every faithful minister serving on the frontlines of Your kingdom. Lord, I decree divine renewal over their bodies, minds, and spirits. Where there has been exhaustion, release supernatural energy. Where there has been heaviness, let the wind of the Spirit lift them to higher places.

Father, strengthen their inner man. Let the power of Your might overshadow them so completely that discouragement finds no place. I call forth resilience, perseverance, and unshakable faith to arise in their hearts. They will run their race with endurance and finish their course with joy.

Lord, as they wait upon You in prayer, meditation, and worship, let divine refreshing flood their souls. Raise them up above every storm of ministry challenges and personal battles. Like eagles soaring above the wind, let them gain new perspectives, renewed vision, and supernatural strategies to lead Your people.

Where weariness has tried to break them, I decree renewed vigor. Where opposition has come against them, I declare unshakable victory. Let their feet be swift with purpose, their hands strong for the work, and their spirits filled with holy fire.

Today, I speak over my pastor and all ministers of the Gospel: They will run and not grow weary. They will walk and not faint. Their strength will be continually renewed by the Lord of Hosts.

In Jesus' name, Amen.

DAY 25

HEALING AND FRUITFULNESS COVENANT

"You shall serve Yahweh your God, and he will bless your bread and your water, and I will take sickness away from among you. No one will miscarry or be barren in your land. I will fulfill the number of your days."
— Exodus 23:25–26 WEB

Mighty Deliverer, Covenant-Keeping God, today I decree this promise over my pastor and every servant in Your vineyard: As they serve You with all their hearts, You will bless their bread, their water, their health, their homes, and their entire households.

I cry out for divine immunity upon their bodies. Let sickness be far from them. I silence every assignment of premature death, disease, and infirmity sent against them. By the blood of Jesus, I decree long life, strength, and vitality over every minister faithfully laboring in the Gospel.

Father, bless their homes with fruitfulness—spiritual fruit, physical health, emotional well-being, and family increase. Let barrenness be broken in every area of their lives. Where joy has been stolen, restore it in double measure.

Lord, honor the covenant of longevity over their lives. Fulfill the number of their days as ordained before the foundation of the world. They will not die before their time; they will live to declare Your works from generation to generation.

Today, I prophetically declare an atmosphere of health, strength, and supernatural refreshing around every pastor and minister. Their homes will be places of laughter, peace, and covenant blessing as they continue to serve You with undivided hearts.

In Jesus' name, Amen.

DAY 26

PEACE BEYOND UNDERSTANDING

> "In nothing be anxious, but in everything, by prayer and petition with thanksgiving, let your requests be made known to God. And the peace of God, which surpasses all understanding, will guard your hearts and your thoughts in Christ Jesus."
> — Philippians 4:6–7 WEB

Prince of Peace, I lift up my pastor and every laborer in Your vineyard before Your throne today. Lord, I decree that anxiety, fear, and turmoil will have no hold over their minds or emotions. Let divine peace, beyond human comprehension, guard their hearts and minds like a mighty fortress.

Father, where ministry burdens have weighed heavily, I release supernatural rest. Where pressures have mounted from finances, family needs, or spiritual warfare, let Your peace intervene with power and assurance.

I pray for a fresh baptism of joy and thanksgiving over their lives. As they lift up their prayers to You, let answers come swiftly, breakthroughs manifest visibly, and testimonies overflow abundantly.

Lord, silence every storm of confusion around them. Let the stillness of Your presence become their hiding place. From the pulpit to their private lives, surround them with a peace that disarms the enemy and strengthens their hearts.

Today, I decree that my pastor and ministers worldwide will walk in unshakable peace. Anxiety will bow, fear will scatter, and divine serenity will reign in every decision, every sermon, every family matter, and every personal battle.

In Jesus' name, Amen.

DAY 27

CONFIDENCE IN GOD'S REFUGE

"In the fear of Yahweh is a secure fortress, and he will be a
refuge for his children."
— Proverbs 14:26 WEB

Lord God Almighty, my Refuge and Strong Tower, today I lift my
voice in prophetic intercession over my pastor and every servant of
the Gospel around the world. May the fear of the Lord anchor their
lives, making You their everlasting refuge and fortress.

Father, let them find safety under the shadow of Your wings. Where
attacks of the enemy have risen like floods, be their strong defense.
Where discouragement has knocked at their doors, let Your Word
fortify their spirits with courage and boldness.

I decree that their children will grow up secure in Your love,
shielded from every arrow of the wicked one. Let the legacy of faith
in their families be unshakable, a heritage of righteousness that
stands for generations.

Lord, turn every battle into victory and every test into a testimony.
From their health to their homes, let divine protection surround
them as walls of fire. May no weapon formed against them prosper,
and every tongue rising in judgment be silenced by the power of
Your name.

Today, I declare that my pastor and all ministers of the Gospel will
dwell in safety, walk in wisdom, and experience the refuge of the

Almighty in every season of life and ministry. In Jesus' name, Amen.

WEEK 5: CHURCH GROWTH, IMPACT & KINGDOM ADVANCE

The Gospel must run swiftly, transforming lives and shaping nations. Pastors and ministers are carriers of this mandate, and the Church is God's chosen vessel for Kingdom expansion. This week, our intercession will target supernatural growth, spiritual influence, and harvest of souls through their ministries. We will declare open doors for evangelism, discipleship, and impact in communities and nations. Our prayers will call forth laborers for the harvest, resources for the vision, and a mighty wave of revival power sweeping through churches. As we travail in prayer, the Kingdom will advance forcefully, and Christ's name will be glorified worldwide.

DAY 28

THE LORD OF THE HARVEST

"The harvest indeed is plentiful, but the laborers are few.
Pray therefore that the Lord of the harvest will send out
laborers into his harvest."
— Matthew 9:37–38 WEB

O Lord of the Harvest, King of Glory, I lift my voice in prophetic intercession before Your throne! You, who reign over the nations and the hearts of men, have declared the fields are ripe for harvest. Today, I stand in the gap for my pastor and for every laborer called to this holy assignment. Father, let fresh strength descend upon them like rain upon thirsty ground.

I decree that no assignment given to them by Your Spirit will be left undone because of lack of willing and equipped laborers. Send forth men and women anointed with wisdom, courage, and fire to stand beside my pastor in the great harvest of souls. Raise up those who will not faint under the weight of ministry but will run with endurance, empowered by the Holy Spirit.

Lord, break the grip of weariness and discouragement from every shepherd laboring in Your fields. I call forth supernatural helpers—sons and daughters of the Kingdom—who will uphold the arms of Your servants as they gather the end-time harvest. May pastors across the nations never labor alone but be surrounded by workers who carry Your burden with joy.

I declare that no harvest will rot in the field because of a shortage of laborers. From my pastor's ministry to the farthest corners of the earth, let there be an overflow of trained, willing, and Spirit-filled hands ready for the work.

Father, I prophesy multiplication, fruitfulness, and unstoppable advance in the Kingdom because You, the Lord of the Harvest, are sending help even now. In Jesus' name, Amen.

DAY 29

DAILY INCREASE AND FAVOR

> "Day by day, continuing steadfastly with one accord in the temple, and breaking bread at home, they took their food with gladness and singleness of heart, praising God and having favor with all the people. The Lord added to the assembly day by day those who were being saved."
> — Acts 2:46–47 WEB

Mighty God of Pentecost fire, I lift my voice in prophetic intercession today, crying out for my pastor and every minister of the Gospel who labors faithfully in Your vineyard. Just as the early Church burned with zeal and multiplied daily, so let there be divine acceleration and increase in their ministries!

I decree that the Spirit of unity and singleness of heart that marked the early believers will rest upon my pastor's congregation and upon churches across the globe. Let the walls of division crumble, and let the Church rise as one body, one voice, one mission. Where there has been strife or stagnation, release a fresh wind of harmony and purpose, O Lord.

Father, I prophesy supernatural favor upon my pastor and fellow ministers before communities, cities, and nations. As they lift up the name of Jesus in word and deed, let doors of influence swing wide open. I declare that hearts long closed to the Gospel will be softened and transformed by the power of Your Spirit.

Lord, let their labor produce fruit that remains. As in the book of Acts, may souls be added daily—yes, daily!—to the Kingdom through their preaching, teaching, and outreach. Multiply the impact of every sermon, every prayer, every act of obedience.

I call forth a season of divine increase, where ministries overflow with testimonies of salvation, healing, and transformation. Let revival fire burn unhindered across the nations through Your faithful servants. In Jesus' name, Amen.

DAY 30

GOD GIVES THE GROWTH

"I planted. Apollos watered. But God gave the increase. So then neither he who plants is anything, nor he who waters, but God who gives the increase."
— 1 Corinthians 3:6–7 WEB

Eternal God, the One who gives the increase, I come before Your throne with prophetic passion today, interceding for my pastor and for every servant who labors in Your Kingdom. Lord, I recognize that human effort alone cannot produce lasting fruit; it is Your Spirit who brings the harvest.

Father, I declare that every seed of the Word sown by my pastor will take root in the hearts of men and women. As they labor in preaching, teaching, counseling, and leading, let there be divine multiplication beyond what human eyes can see. May the waterers be faithful, the planters diligent, but above all, let Your power bring supernatural results.

I decree that pride, striving, and discouragement will not hinder the work of ministry. My pastor and fellow ministers will rest in the assurance that growth belongs to You alone. Break the yoke of performance-driven burdens, and let them minister from a place of Spirit-led obedience, knowing You bring the increase.

Lord, where ministries have toiled with little visible fruit, I call forth a sudden season of breakthrough and expansion. Let congregations overflow, disciples multiply, and the Gospel advance swiftly across cities and nations because You, O Lord, are at work.

I prophesy that the hands of Your servants will never labor in vain. The seeds they plant today will yield harvests for generations to come, for You, the God of increase, are faithful to fulfill Your word. In Jesus' name, Amen.

DAY 31

NATIONS SHALL COME

"Arise, shine; for your light has come, and Yahweh's glory
has risen on you. For, behold, darkness will cover the
earth, and deep darkness the peoples; but Yahweh will
arise on you, and his glory shall be seen on you. Nations
will come to your light, and kings to the brightness of your
rising."
— Isaiah 60:1–3 WEB

Glorious King of Glory, I lift my voice in prophetic intercession,
declaring over my pastor and every minister of the Gospel: Arise
and shine! The hour has come for the Church to stand in radiant
power and authority, for the glory of the Lord rests upon His
servants.

Father, I decree that no darkness of discouragement, opposition, or
limitation will overshadow the ministries of Your servants. Where
the enemy has tried to suppress the light of the Gospel, let there
now be an uncontainable shining forth of Your glory. Nations and
leaders shall witness the power of Christ in their lives and be drawn
to the brightness of their rising.

Lord, I call forth supernatural influence for pastors across the globe.
May kings, presidents, governors, and communities seek the
wisdom and counsel of Your servants because of the undeniable
presence of God upon them. Let the light of Christ in their
ministries break cultural, political, and spiritual barriers.

I prophesy that entire cities and nations will be shaken by the light of the Gospel flowing through their preaching, teaching, and outreach. As they arise in obedience, let revival break forth like the dawn, scattering darkness and establishing the Kingdom of God.

Father, cause their ministries to radiate with Your glory, drawing souls from every tribe, tongue, and nation into Your marvelous light. The Church will shine brighter than ever before because the glory of the Lord has risen upon her. In Jesus' name, Amen.

EPILOGUE

The call to intercede for spiritual leaders is not casual; it is a sacred responsibility. As you close this book, I challenge you to carry forward what you have begun here—not as a thirty-one-day exercise, but as a lifestyle of relentless, Spirit-led intercession. Pastors and ministers cannot stand alone. Every sermon preached, every life counseled, every prayer offered by them carries eternal weight—and the enemy is relentless in his pursuit to weaken, distract, and discourage them. Your prayers are the frontlines of defense.

This is more than ritual; it is partnership with God's purposes. It is standing in the gap when the burden is too heavy, speaking words of authority when the enemy seeks to sow confusion, and releasing Heaven's resources when ministries face lack. Your intercession is prophetic, powerful, and transformational—it shapes destinies, influences nations, and strengthens the hands of those laboring in the fields of eternity.

I challenge you to go beyond these pages. Pray without ceasing. Lift up pastors, mentors, and spiritual leaders with persistence, faith, and courage. Let your heart break for their burdens and rise for their victories. Let your prayers become a voice that the heavens cannot ignore.

The world may not always recognize their sacrifice, but Heaven does. And when you join in prayer for them, you are partnering with God Himself to release strength, protection, wisdom, and blessing. Stand boldly, pray fiercely, and intercede faithfully. The Kingdom will advance, the Church will flourish, and the laborers you lift will stand strong because of the prayers you refuse to withhold.

In Jesus' name, Amen.

ENCOURAGE OTHERS WITH YOUR STORY

If this prayer guide has strengthened your faith, deepened your intercession, or helped you stand in the gap, would you consider leaving a short review on Amazon? Your feedback not only encourages others but also helps more believers discover this resource and join in the prayer movement. Every review—just a few sentences—makes a difference. Thank you for being part of this movement.

MORE FROM PRAYERSCRIPTS

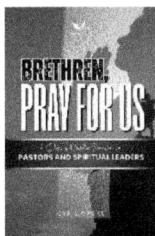

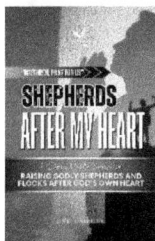

Command Your Morning:

30 Days of Prayers and Declarations to Seize Your Day and Shape Your Destiny

There is a battle over every morning—and every believer must choose to either drift into the day or command it.

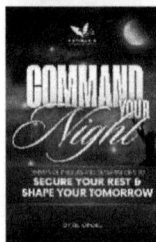

Command Your Night:

30 Days of Prayers and Declarations to Secure Your Rest and Shape Your Tomorrow

Every night is a spiritual battlefield—what you do before you sleep can determine the course of your tomorrow.

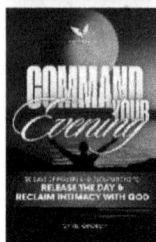

Command Your Evening:

30 Days of Prayers and Declarations to Release the Day and Reclaim Intimacy with God

There is a battle over every transition—and evening is one of the most spiritually neglected.

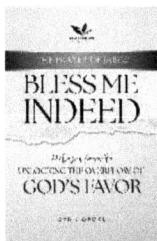

Bless Me Indeed:

Unlocking the Overflow of God's Favor

What if you could activate God's favor in your life today and walk in blessings that surpass your wildest expectations?

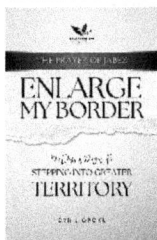

Enlarge My Border:

Stepping Into Greater Territory

Do you feel like you're living beneath your full potential? Do limitations, setbacks, and invisible barriers keep you from stepping into all God has promised? It's time to lift your cry for enlargement.

May Your Hand Be With Me:

Living Under Divine Power and Presence

What happens when the mighty hand of God rests upon your life? Doors open that no man can shut. Strength rises where weakness once prevailed. Guidance comes in the midst of confusion, and protection surrounds you in every battle.

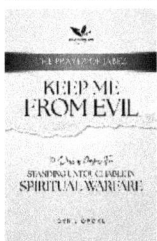

Keep Me From Evil:

Standing Untouchable in Spiritual Warfare

What if the enemy's plans could never touch you or your family? Imagine walking through life completely protected, untouchable, and victorious—no matter what schemes are formed against you.

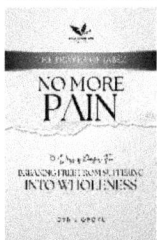

No More Pain:

Breaking Free from Suffering into Wholeness

Have you been carrying the weight of sorrow, disappointment, or hidden wounds for far too long? Do cycles of pain seem to repeat in your life, your marriage, or your family?

Discern the Enemy:

Sharpening Spiritual Perception to Recognize Satan's Tactics and Guard Your Destiny

The greatest danger is not the enemy you can see—it is the one you cannot. Can you recognize the enemy before he strikes?

Disarm the Enemy:

Stripping Satan of Weapons and Influence Through the Power of Christ

Are you tired of feeling like the enemy has the upper hand in your life? It's time to take back your ground, silence the lies of darkness, and walk in the unstoppable authority of Christ.

Destroy the Enemy:

Breaking Strongholds and Cancelling Evil Works by God's Authority

Are you tired of living under the weight of unseen battles? It's time to rise up and destroy the enemy's works in your life.

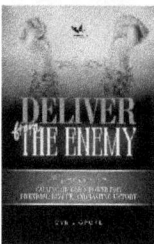

Deliver from the Enemy:

Calling on God's Power for Freedom, Rescue, and Lasting Victory

Break free from spiritual attacks and experience God's mighty deliverance in every battle.

Declare Against the Enemy:

Speaking God's Word Boldly to Enforce Triumph Over Darkness

What if you could silence the enemy's schemes, protect your family, and walk boldly into every God-ordained assignment with unshakable authority?

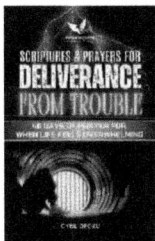

Scriptures & Prayers for Deliverance from Trouble:

40 Days of Prayer for When Life Feels Overwhelming

Are you walking through a season where life feels heavy and your prayers feel weak?

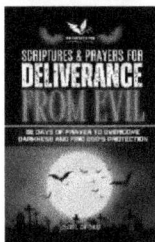

Scriptures & Prayers for Deliverance from Evil:

50 Days of Prayer to Overcome Darkness and Find God's Protection

When darkness presses in, how do you pray?

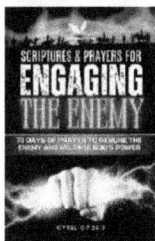

Scriptures & Prayers for Engaging the Enemy:

70 Days of Prayer to Rebuke the Enemy and Release God's Power

You weren't called to run from the battle—you were anointed to win it.

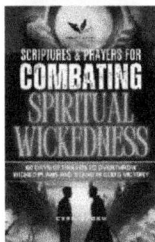

Scriptures & Prayers for Combating Spiritual Wickedness:

50 Days of Prayer to Overthrow Wicked Plans and Stand in God's Victory

Are you facing opposition that feels deeper than the natural? You're not imagining it—and you're not powerless.

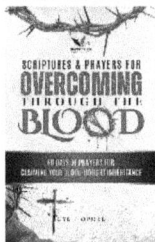

Scriptures & Prayers for Overcoming Through the Blood:

60 Days of Prayers for Claiming Your Blood-Bought Inheritance

You were never meant to fight sin, fear, or Satan in your own strength.

Standing in the Gap for Covenant Awakening:

30 Days of Prayer for National Repentance, Righteous Leadership & God's Sovereign Rule

What if your prayers could help turn the tide of a nation?

Standing in the Gap for Divine Defense:

30 Days of Prayer for National Guidance, Guarding & Glory

When the foundations of a nation feel as if they're shaking, prayer is the strongest fortress you can build.

Standing in the Gap for National Healing:

40 Days of Prayer for Reconciliation, Righteousness, and Restoration

What if your prayers could help heal a nation? What if God is waiting for someone—like you—to stand in the gap?

Standing in the Gap for The President:

50 Days of Prayer for Leadership, Loyalty, and Lifeline

When a nation's leader is under spiritual siege, will you answer the call to stand in the gap?

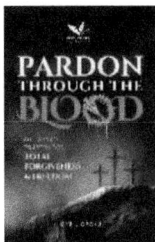

Pardon Through the Blood:

60 Days of Prayers for Total Forgiveness and Freedom

Guilt is a prison. The blood of Jesus holds the key.

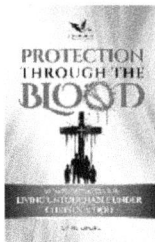

Protection Through the Blood:

60 Days of Prayers for Living Untouchable Under Christ's Blood

You are not helpless. You are not exposed. You are covered—completely—by the blood of Jesus.

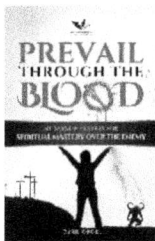

Prevail Through the Blood:

60 Days of Prayers for Spiritual Mastery Over the Enemy

What if every scheme of the enemy against your life could be dismantled—by one unstoppable weapon?

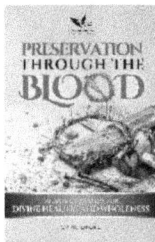

Preservation Through the Blood:

60 Days of Prayers for Divine Healing and Wholeness

Unlock Lasting Healing and Wholeness Through the Blood of Jesus

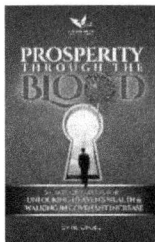

Prosperity Through the Blood:

60 Days of Prayers for Unlocking Heaven's Wealth and Walking in Covenant Increase

You were redeemed for more than survival—you were redeemed to prosper.

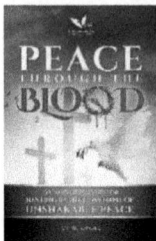

Peace Through the Blood:

60 Days of Prayers for Resting in the Covenant of Unshakable Peace

Are you ready to silence every storm of the mind, heart, and home—once and for all?

www.ingramcontent.com/pod-product-compliance
Lightning Source LLC
Chambersburg PA
CBHW062019040426
42447CB00010B/2063